ACRES OF DIAMONDS

T0160169

ACRES OF DIAMONDS

by Russell H. Conwell

*The Classic Work on
Finding Your Fortune
Where You Least Expect It*

Abridged and Introduced
by Mitch Horowitz

THE CONDENSED CLASSICS LIBRARY

Published by Gildan Media LLC
aka G&D Media.
www.GandDmedia.com

Acres of Diamonds was originally delivered as a lecture and appeared in book form in 1890.
This abridgement is from editions published in 1901 and 1925.
G&D Media Condensed Classics edition published 2018
Abridgement and Introduction copyright © 2016 by Mitch Horowitz

FIRST EDITION: 2018

Cover design by David Rheinhardt of Pyrographx

Interior design by Meghan Day Healey of Story Horse, LLC.

ISBN: 978-1-7225-0056-6

Contents

Serve and Grow Rich

Author Russell H. Conwell belonged to a generation of late nineteenth-century motivational writers who regarded good character as the indispensible ingredient to success. Without character, the minister and educator said, you could attain no success worthy of the name.

Conwell began giving his famous lecture *Acres of Diamonds* in the 1870s, and was said to have delivered it more than 6,152 times around the nation before his death in 1925. He maintained a grueling speaking schedule not only to encourage young people in the ways of ethical achievement, but also to use his speaking fees to found a college dedicated to placing education in reach of working-class students. That school today is Temple University in Philadelphia.

Acres of Diamonds remains as sturdy a guide to life as when Conwell first received inspiration for the lecture (and its title) while traveling as a journalist through Persia and Northern Africa in 1869. The ex-Civil War officer spent many hours (not always happily) listening to folk stories that his Arab guides insisted on reciting for travellers. One of the guides told him an intriguing morality tale about a wealthy Persian farmer who had squandered his money and life searching the world for diamonds—dying a pauper before diamonds were finally discovered, on the very farm that he had abandoned to embark on his quest.

The lesson that Conwell took from this story forms the heart of *Acres of Diamonds*: Success can be found right where you stand—provided you possess the simplicity and soundness of character to see it. While *Acres of Diamonds* holds many lessons for today's success-hungry reader, it differs in tone from later generations of motivational literature. Conwell insisted that good character and good business are innately joined: one could not exist without the other. The chief aim of the good businessman, he taught, is to figure out what the people around you need, and devote yourself to filling those needs. This can also make you very wealthy.

Conwell did not believe that it was the job of the capitalist to fleece his customers and workers, but rather to profit from them on the same scale as they profited from him. "I should sell each bill of goods," Conwell wrote, "so that the person to whom I sell shall make as much as I make."

Conwell's book made a surprising return to the news in 2015 when high-tech entrepreneur Dan Price responded to the national rise in income inequality by announcing a minimum salary of $70,000 for workers at his Seattle credit-card processing firm. Price's move generated headlines and controversy. "If there was a 19th-century thinker Mr. Price drew inspiration from," wrote *The New York Times*, "it would be not Karl Marx, but Russell Conwell, the Baptist minister and Temple University founder, whose famed 'Acres of Diamonds' speech fused Christianity and capitalism."

The *Times* was right. Conwell saw the good Christian and the good businessman as one and the same, though he noted that his ideas were for motivated people of all backgrounds.

In this condensed edition of *Acres of Diamonds*, be on the lookout for four principles, which form the foundation of Conwell's success philosophy:

1. Greatness is achieved where you are.
2. Success, including wealth, comes from *filling a human need*.
3. The truly great are *simple*—in speech, methods, ideas, and inventions.

4. Money is power, greatness, and good—but only in the hands someone who will *use it well.*

Although Conwell's examples often focused on entrepreneurship, his principles can be used in any job or pursuit. Conwell's ideal of success—as radical today as it was in the Victorian age—boils down to this: If you sincerely care enough about people to understand and provide for their needs, you will receive material rewards, which, in turn, can be used to uplift others. This is the circle of sound business, good ethics, and meaningful existence.

—Mitch Horowitz

Acres of Diamonds

The title of this lecture originated in 1869. My travelling party and I had hired a guide from Baghdad to take us down the Tigris River to the Arabian Gulf. Our guide resembled the barbers found in America. That is, he resembled the barbers in certain mental characteristics. He thought it was not only his duty to guide us down the river, but also to entertain us with stories: curious and weird, ancient and modern, strange and familiar. Many of them I have forgotten, and I am glad that I have. But there is one that has stayed with me always.

At a certain point in our journey, the guide had grown irritable over my lack of appreciation for his tales. As he led my camel by the halter he introduced a new story by saying: "This is a tale that I reserve for my *particular friends*." He immediately had my close attention.

He then told me that there once lived near the shore of the River Indus, toward which we were travelling, an ancient Persian by the name of Ali Hafed. He said that Ali Hafed owned a large farm, with orchards, grain fields, and gardens; that he loaned money at interest; had a beautiful wife and lovely children; and was a wealthy and contented man.

One day there visited this old Persian farmer one of those ancient Buddhist priests, one of the wise men of the East, who sat down by Ali Hafed's fireside and told the farmer how this world was created in fascinating—and not unscientific—detail. The priest concluded by telling the farmer that a diamond was the last and the highest of God's mineral creations. The old priest told Ali Hafed that if the farmer had a diamond the size of his thumb, he could purchase a dozen farms like his.

"And," said the priest, "if you had a handful of diamonds, you could purchase the county, and if you had a mine of diamonds you could purchase kingdoms."

Ali Hafed heard all about diamonds that night—and went to bed a poor man in his mind. He wanted a whole mine of diamonds. Early in the morning he sought out the priest.

"Will you tell me where I can find diamonds?" Ali Hafed asked.

"Diamonds?" the priest said. "What do you want of diamonds?"

"I want to be immensely rich," said Ali Hafed.

"Well," said the priest, "if you want diamonds, all you have to do is go find them, and then you will have them."

"But I don't know where to go," said Ali Hafed.

"If you will find a river that runs over white sands between high mountains, in those white sands you will always find diamonds," replied the priest.

"But," asked Ali Hafed, do you believe there is such a place?"

"Plenty of them," said the priest. "You just have to go where they are."

So, Ali Hafed sold his farm, left his family in charge of a neighbor, and away he went in search of diamonds.

He began at the mountain range at the source of the Nile River. Afterward he went to the Holy Land, and then into Europe. At last, when his money was all gone and he was in rags and starving, he stood on the shores at Barcelona in Spain, and he cast himself into the incoming tide, sank beneath its foaming crest, never to rise in this life again.

When the old Arab guide told me this story he stopped to rearrange some of our belongings and I had an opportunity to muse over what he had said. I asked myself: "Why did this old guide reserve this story for his *particular friends*?" But when he began again I discovered that this was the first story that I had ever heard where the hero died in the first chapter—for the guide began a second chapter just as though there had been no break.

The guide went on to say that the man who had purchased Ali Hafed's farm led his camel out into the garden to drink, and as the animal put his nose into the shallow waters of the garden brook, Ali Hafed's successor noticed a curious flash of light from the white sands of the stream. Reaching in he pulled out a black stone containing a strange eye of light. He took it into the house as a curiosity, placed it on the mantel, and forgot about it.

Not long after that same old priest came to visit Ali Hafed's successor. The moment he stepped in the room he noticed the flash of light. The priest rushed to the mantel and said: "Here is a diamond! Here is a diamond! Has Ali Hafed returned?"

"Oh no, Ali Hafed has not returned and we have not heard from him," the new owner said. "And that is not a diamond; it is nothing but a stone we found out in our garden."

"But I know a diamond when I see one," said the priest, "and *that* is a diamond."

Together they rushed out into the garden. They stirred up the white sands, and came upon other more beautiful, more valuable gems than the first.

In this way, said the guide—and, friends, it is historically true—was discovered the diamond mines of Golconda, the most valuable diamond mines in the ancient world.

Well, when the guide had finished the second chapter to his story he took off his cap and swung it in the air to call attention to the moral. He said to me: "Had Ali Hafed remained at home, and dug in his own cellar, or underneath his own wheat field, instead of wretchedness, starvation, poverty, and death in a strange land, he would have had *acres of diamonds*."

When the guide added his moral I saw why he reserved the story for his *particular friends.* I didn't tell him that I could see it. He had a way of going around a thing, like a lawyer, and saying indirectly what he didn't dare say directly: That in his personal opinion there was a certain young man travelling down the Tigris River who might be better off at home in America.

I told him that his tale reminded me of one. I told him that a man in Northern California owned a ranch in 1847. The rancher heard they had discovered gold in Southern California, though they had not. He sold his ranch to Colonel John Sutter, who put a mill on the little stream below the house. One day the next year, his little girl gathered some of the sand in her hands at the raceway, and brought it into the house. While she was sifting it through her fingers, a visitor noticed the first shining scales of real gold that were ever discovered in California. Acres and acres of gold.

But before we judge the unfortunate California rancher, or poor Ali Hafed, keep in mind that you and I have done the same as they. Ah, now you will say: "Oh no, I never had any acres of diamonds or gold mines." But I say to you that you *did* have gold mines and acres of diamonds—and you have them right now.

Now, let me speak with the greatest care lest my eccentricity of manner should mislead my listeners, and make you think that I am here to entertain more than to help. I want to hold your attention with sufficient interest to leave my lesson with you.

You have had an opportunity to become rich; and to some of you it has been a hardship to purchase a ticket to this lecture. You have no right to be poor. It is all wrong. You have no right to be poor. It is your duty to be rich.

You ought to make money. Money is power, and you ought to be reasonably ambitious to have it. You ought to because you can do more good with it than you could without it. Money printed your Bible, money builds your churches, money sends your missionaries, money pays your preachers, and you would not have many of them, either, if you did not pay them.

Think of how much good you could do if you had money now. Again, money is power—and it ought to be in the hands of good men. It would be in the hands of good men if we comply with Scripture, in which God promises prosperity to the righteous man. That means more than being goody-goody—it means the all-around righteous man. You should be a righteous man, and if you were, you would be rich.

"Oh," you will say, "Mr. Conwell, can you, as a Christian teacher, tell the young people to spend their lives making money? Don't you think there are some things in this world that are better than money?"

Of course I do, but I am talking about money now. Of course there are some things higher than money. Oh, yes, I know by the grave that has left me standing alone that there are some things in this world that are higher and sweeter and purer than money. I also know that there is not one of those things that is not greatly enhanced by the use of money. Love is the grandest thing on God's earth, but fortunate the lover who has plenty of money. I say again, money is power, money is force, money will do good, as well as harm. In the hands of good men and women it could accomplish, and has accomplished, good.

I need to guard myself right here. Because one of my theological students came to me once to charge me with heresy inasmuch as I had said that money was power.

He said: "Mr. Conwell, I feel it my duty to tell you that Scripture says that money 'is the root of all evil.'"

I said: "I would like you to find that passage for me. I have never seen it."

He triumphantly brought a Bible, and with all the bigoted pride of a narrow sectarian, who founds his creed on some misinterpretation of Scripture, threw it down before me and said: "There it is!" And he read: "The *love* of money is the root of all evil."

Indeed it is. The *love* of money is the root of all evil. The love of money—rather than the love of the good it secures—*is* a dangerous evil in the community. The desire to grab hold of money, and to hold onto it, "hugging the dollar until the eagle squeals," is the root of all evil. But it is a grand ambition for men to desire money that they may use it for the benefit of their fellow men.

I say to you, then, that you ought to be rich.

"Well," you say, "I would like to be rich, but I have never had an opportunity. I have never had any diamonds about me!"

My friends you did have an opportunity. And let us see where your mistake was.

What business have you been in?

"Oh," some man or woman will say, "I keep a store on one of these side streets, and I am so far from the great commercial center that I cannot make any money."

"How long have you kept that store?"

"Twenty years."

"Twenty years and not turning a handsome profit now? There is something wrong with you. Nothing wrong with the side street. It is with you."

"Oh now," you will say, "anybody knows that you must be in the center of trade if you are going to make money."

The man of common sense will not admit that that is necessarily true at all. If you are keeping that store and you are not making money, it would have been better for the community if they had kicked you out of that store nineteen years ago.

No man has a right to go into business and not make money. It is a crime to go into business and lose money, because it is a curse to the rest of the community. No man has a moral right to transact business unless he makes something out of it. He has also no right to transact business unless the man he deals with has an opportunity to make something. Unless he lives and lets live, he is not an honest man in business. There are no exceptions to this great rule.

You ought to have been rich. You have no right to keep a store for twenty years and still be poor. You will say to me: "Now, Mr. Conwell, I know the mercantile business better than you do."

My friend, let us consider this a minute.

When I was young my father kept a country store in western Massachusetts, and once in while he left me in charge of that store. Fortunately for him it was not often. When I had it in my charge a man came in the door and asked: "Do you keep jackknives?"

"No, we don't keep jackknives." Then I went off and whistled a tune, and what did I care for that man?

Then another man would come in the same door and say, "Do you keep jackknives?"

"No, we don't keep jackknives." Then I went off and whistled another tune, and what did I care for that man?

Then another man would come in that same door and say, "Do you keep jackknives?"

"No, we don't keep jackknives. Do you suppose we are keeping this store just for the purpose of supplying the whole neighborhood with jackknives?"

Do you carry on your business like that? Do you ask what was the problem with it? The problem was that I had not learned that the foundational principles of business success and the foundational principles of

Christianity are both the same. It is the whole of every man's life to be doing for his fellow men. And he who can do the most to help his fellow men is entitled to the greatest reward himself. Not only so says God's holy book, but so says every man's business common sense.

If I had been carrying on my father's store on a Christian plan, or on a plan that leads to success, I would have had a jackknife for the third man when he called for it. Then I would have actually done him a kindness, and I would have received a reward myself, which it would have been my duty to take.

There are some overly pious Christians who think that if you take any profit on anything you sell that you are an unrighteous man. On the contrary, you would be a criminal to sell goods for less than they cost. You have no right to do that. You cannot trust a man with your money who cannot take care of his own. You cannot trust a man in your family who is not true to his own wife. You cannot trust a man in the world who does not begin with his own heart, his own character, his own life.

It would have been my duty to have furnished a jackknife to the third man, or the second, and to have sold it to him and actually profited myself. I have no more right to sell goods without making a profit on them than I have to overcharge dishonestly beyond what they are worth. I should sell each bill of goods so that the person to whom I sell shall make as much as I make.

To live and let live is the principle of the gospel, and the principle of everyday common sense. Oh young man, hear me: live as you go along. Do not wait until you have reached my years before you begin to enjoy anything in life. The man who has gone through life dividing fairly with his fellow men, making and demanding his own rights and his own profits, and given to every other man his rights and profits, lives every day, and not only that, but he is on the royal road to wealth.

But you say: "I don't carry on my business like you did back in Massachusetts." But if you have not made any money, you are carrying on your business like that, and I can tell you what you will say to me tomorrow morning when I go into your store.

I come to you and ask: "Do you know Mr. A?"

"Oh yes. He lives up in the next block. He shops here at my little store."

"Well, where is he originally from?"

"I don't know."

"Does he own his own house?"

"I don't know."

"What business is he in?"

"I don't know."

"Do his children go to school?"

"I don't know."

"What party does he vote?"

"I don't know."

"What church does he go to?"

"I don't know, and I don't care."

Do you answer me like that tomorrow morning in your store? Then you are carrying on your business just as I carried on my father's business back in Massachusetts.

You don't know where Mr. A came from and you *don't care*. You don't care whether he has a happy home. You don't know what church he attends, and you don't care! If you had cared, you would have been a rich man right now.

You never thought it was part of your duty to help him make money. So you cannot succeed! You are acting against every law of business and every rule of political economy, and failure is guaranteed and deserved. What right have you to be in business taking no interest in your fellow men, and not endeavoring to supply them with what they need? You cannot succeed.

I know of a merchant in Boston who made millions of dollars and who began his enterprises out in the suburbs where there were not a dozen houses on the street; although there were other stores scattered about. He became such a necessity to the neighborhood that when he wished to move into the city, the community came to him with a great petition, signed by all the people, begging him not to close that store. He had always looked after the community's interests. He had always carefully studied what they wanted and advised them rightly. He was a necessity; and they must make him wealthy; for in proportion as you are of use to fellow men, in that proportion can they afford to pay you.

You are poor because you are not wanted. You should have made yourself a necessity to the world, and the world would have paid you your own price.

Young man, remember: if you are going to invest your life or talent or money, you must look around and see what people need and then invest yourself, or your money, in that which they need most. Then will your fortune be made, for they must take care of you. It is a difficult lesson to learn.

Why does one merchant surpass another? Why does one manufacturer outsell another? It is simply because that one has found out what people want, and does not waste his time or money on things they do not need. That is the whole of it. A great merchant once said: "I am not going to buy things people do not want. I will take an interest in people and study their needs."

"But," you will say, "I cannot do that here." Yes you can. It is being done in smaller places now, and you can do it as well as another.

The farmer will be more successful when he gives more attention to what people want and not so much to what will grow, though he needs them both. But now the whole time of most of our farmers is taken up with the finding out of "what will grow."

Who are the great inventors? Always the men who are the simplest and plainest. The great inventor has the simple mind, and invents the simplest machine. Did you ever think how simple the first telephones and the telegraph were? The simplest mind is always the greatest. Did you ever see a great man? Great in every noble and true sense? If so, you could walk right up to him and say, "How are you, Jim?" Just think of the great men you have met and you find this is true.

When I was an officer in the Civil War one my soldiers had been sentenced to death for desertion. I went up to the White House—sent there for the first time in my life—to see the President and petition for the boy's life.

I went into the waiting room and sat down with a lot of others on the benches, and the secretary asked one after another to tell him what they wanted. After the secretary had been through the line, he went in, and then came back to the door and motioned for me. I went up to that anteroom, and the secretary said: "That is the president's door right over there. Just rap on it and go right in."

I was never so taken aback in all my life, never. The secretary himself made it worse for me, because he had told me how to go in and then went out another door to the left and shut that. There I was, in the hallway by myself before the President of the United States of America's door. I had been on fields of battle, where the shells did sometimes shriek and the bullets did sometimes hit me, but I always wanted to run. I have no sympathy with the old man who says, "I would just as soon march up to the cannon's mouth as eat my dinner." I have no faith in a man who doesn't know enough to be afraid when he is being shot at. I never was so afraid when the shells came around us at Antietam as I was when I went into that room that day; but I finally mustered the courage—I don't know how I ever did—and at arm's length tapped on the door. The man inside did not help me at all, but yelled out: "Come in and sit down!"

Well, I went in and sat down on the edge of a chair, and wished I were in Europe. The man at the table did not look up. He was one of the world's greatest men, and was great by one single rule. Oh, that I could say this one thing to all the young people of our nation, and that they would remember it. I would give a lifetime for the effect it would have on our community and on our civilization. Abraham Lincoln's principle for greatness can be adopted by nearly all. This was his rule: Whatever he had to do at all, he put his whole mind into it and held it all there until he was done. That makes men great almost anywhere. He stuck to those papers at that table and did not look up at me, and I sat there trembling.

Finally, when he had put the string around his papers, he pushed them over to one side and looked over to me, and a smile came over his worn face. He said: "I am a very busy man and have only a few minutes to spare. Now tell me in the fewest words what it is you want."

I began to tell him, and mentioned the case, and he said: "I have heard all about it and you do not need to say any more. Mr. Stanton"—his secretary of war— "was talking to me only a few days ago about that. You can go back to the hotel and rest assured that the president never did sign an order to shoot a boy under twenty years of age, and never will. You can say that to his mother anyhow."

Then he said to me, "How is it going in the field?" I said, "We sometimes get discouraged." And he said: "It is all right. We are going to win out now. We are getting very near the light. No man ought to wish to be president of the United States, and I will be glad when I get through; then my son Tad and I are going out to Spring-field, Illinois. I have a bought a farm out there and I don't care if I again earn only twenty-five cents a day. Tad has a mule team, and we are going to plant onions."

Then he asked, "Were you brought up on a farm?" I said, "Yes; in the Berkshire Hills of Massachusetts." He then threw his leg over the corner of the big chair and said, "I have heard many a time, ever since I was young, that up there in those hills you have to sharpen the noses of the sheep in order to get down to the grass between the rocks." He was so familiar, so everyday, so farmer-like, that I felt right at home with him at once.

He then took hold of another roll of paper, and looked up at me and said: "Good morning." I took the hint then and got up and went out. After I had gotten out I could not realize I had seen the President of the United States at all.

Did you ever see a man who struts around alto-gether too large to notice an ordinary working me-chanic? Do you think he is great? He is nothing but a puffed-up balloon, held down by his big feet. There is no greatness there. There may be greatness in self-respect but there is no greatness in feeling above one's fellow men. The simple men are the greatest always.

Once I went up to New Hampshire to lecture and when I returned I said I would never lecture in New

Hampshire again. I told a relative of mine, who was a professor at Harvard: "I was cold all the time I was there and I shivered so much that my teeth shook."

"Why did you shiver?" he asked.

"Because it was cold."

"No, that is not the reason you shivered."

Then I said: "I shivered because I had not bed-clothes enough."

"No, that is not the reason."

"Well," I said, "Professor, you are a scientific man. I am not. I would like to have an expert, scientific opinion of why I shivered."

He arose in his facetious way and said to me: "Young man you shivered because you did not know any better! Did you have in your pocket a two-cent newspaper?"

"Oh, yes, I had a *Herald* and a *Journal*."

"That is it. You had them in your pocket, and if you had spread one newspaper over your sheet when you want to bed, you would've been as a warm as the richest man in America under all his silk coverlids. But you shivered because you didn't know enough to put a two-cent newspaper on your bed, and you had it in your pocket."

It is the power to appreciate the little things that brings success. The greatest inventors are those who see what the people need, and then invent something to fill that need. If you know what people need, you have gotten more knowledge of a fortune than any amount of capital can give you. Indeed, the moment a young man or woman gets more money than he or she has grown to by practical experience, that moment he has gotten a curse. I tell you this great secret: Your wealth is too near to you. You are looking right over it.

And note, too, that greatness does not consist in holding high office or in rank, even in times of war. The office does not make the man. Every great general is credited with many victories he never knew anything about, simply because they were won by his subordinates. But it is unfair to give the credit to a general who did not know anything about it. I tell you if the lightening of heaven had struck out of existence every man who wore shoulder straps in our wars, there would have arisen out of the ranks of our private soldiers just as great men to lead the nation to victory.

Greatness really consists in doing great deeds with little means—in the accomplishment of vast purposes from the private ranks of life—in benefiting one's own neighborhood, in blessing one's own city, the community in which he dwells. There, and there only, is the great test of human goodness and human ability. He who waits for a high office before he does great and noble deeds must fail altogether.

I have learned the lesson from being around men who hold high office that you and I should call no man great simply because he holds an office. Greatness! It is something more than office, more than fame, more than genius! It is the great-heartedness that encloses those in need, reaches down to those below, and lifts them up. May this thought come to every one of the young men and women who hear me speak and abide through future years.

I close with the words of Philip James Bailey. He was not one of our greatest writers, but, after all, in this he was one of our best:

We live in deeds, not years; in thoughts, not breaths;
In feelings, not in figures on a dial.
We should count time by heart-throbs. He most lives
Who thinks most . . .

Oh, friends, if you forget everything else I say, don't forget these two lines; for if you think *two* thoughts where I think *one*, you live twice as much as I do in the same length of time:

. . . He most lives
Who thinks most, feels the noblest, acts the best.

About the Authors

Born in western Massachusetts in 1843, RUSSELL H. CONWELL trained as lawyer, served as an officer in the Union army, and worked as an international journalist. He was ordained and worked as a Baptist minister before founding Temple University in Philadelphia in 1884. Conwell founded the school to educate poor and working-class students, and funded it largely through speaking fees earned from his famous motivational and character-building lecture *Acres of Diamonds*, which he began delivering in the 1870s. Conwell gave the talk more than 6,152 times throughout the nation before his death in 1925. He served as Temple University's first president, and his Conwell School of Theology became the Gordon-Conwell Theological Seminary, one of the largest interdenominational seminaries in the United States.

MITCH HOROWITZ, who abridged and introduced this volume, is the PEN Award-winning author of books including *Occult America* and *The Miracle Club: How Thoughts Become Reality. The Washington Post* says Mitch "treats esoteric ideas and movements with an even-handed intellectual studiousness that is too often lost in today's raised-voice discussions." Follow him @MitchHorowitz.

CPSIA information can be obtained
at www.ICGtesting.com
Printed in the USA
BVHW050817101118
532541BV00018B/99/P